Fanning the Flames of Light

A Study of Ephesians

Wes and Elaine Willis

ACCENT PUBLICATIONS
Colorado Springs, Colorado

Accent Publications
4050 Lee Vance View
P.O. Box 36640
Colorado Springs, Colorado   80936

Copyright © 1993 Accent Publications
Printed in the United States of America

All rights reserved. No portion of this book may be reproduced in any form without the written permission of the publishers, with the exception of brief excerpts in magazine reviews.

Library of Congress catalog Card Number 93-72103

ISBN 0-89636-298-1

Second Printing

CONTENTS

	Introduction to Ephesians	5
1	New Blessings in Christ	7
2	New Wisdom in Christ	15
3	New Life in Christ	21
4	New Relationships in Christ	27
5	New Organism: The Body of Christ	35
6	New Power in Christ	43
7	Believers Ministering Faithfully	51
8	Believers Living Holy Lives	59
9	Believers Living Morally Pure Lives	67
10	Believers Reflecting Spirit-Filled Lives	74
11	Believers Obeying the Spirit	82
12	Believers Living With Spiritual Power	90

Introduction to Ephesians

Who was Paul?

We first meet Paul in Acts 7:58 as an unbeliever whose name is "Saul." In this initial encounter, Saul is a bystander encouraging those who murdered Stephen, the church leader, by watching the coats of the perpetrators. Saul's goal was to eradicate Christianity. According to Acts 9, he was traveling from city to city with Roman letters of authorization to locate Christians and put them in jail for their faith.

Saul's life did an about-face when he encountered the post-ascension Jesus on the road to Damascus where he was marvelously converted. Saul, whose name later changed to Paul, then began to promote Christianity with the same ardor and intensity he had previously devoted to opposing it.

Why did he write Ephesians?

Paul visited Ephesus briefly at the end of his second missionary journey and later spent several years there on his final (third) journey (Acts 18:24—19). He wrote this letter to help the Ephesian believers continue to grow and mature following their excellent start in their Christian walk. Many feel that this letter, written from prison around 60 A.D. and delivered by Tychicus, was intended to be read by believers in surrounding cities as well as those in Ephesus. Thus, Ephesians is often called a circular letter.

The book of Ephesians is somewhat unique because, unlike most other epistles, there seems to be no particular doctrinal error or relational problem that Paul is trying to correct. Rather, the book of Ephesians lays a solid theological foundation for Christianity, and then presents the practical application of that foundation.

Chapters 1—3 describe a believer's position in Christ and the spiritual resources available to every Christian. The first half of the book describes the incredible wealth that believers possess. The second half of the book (chapters 4—6) is an intensely practical explanation of how we should live because of our spiritual position. It describes the daily walk of the believer. Paul clearly demonstrates that there is nothing quite so practical as sound doctrine.

Our prayer is that you will come to a deeper understanding of your priceless inheritance in Christ. But beyond that, we pray that your daily Christian walk will be a walk of vitality and victory. May you experience the full blessing of God that is yours because of your position in Christ.

New Blessings in Christ
EPHESIANS 1:1-14

*T*he deceased millionaire, Howard Hughes, holds a bizarre fascination for many. His incredibly eccentric lifestyle, his compulsive seclusion as he approached the end of his life, and the absence of a will after his death all add to the mysterious aura. Though worth millions of dollars, Hughes reportedly withdrew to the shadowy confines of his bedroom, living solely on soft drinks and prepackaged cupcakes. His twilight existence gave no indication of the abundant resources at his disposal.

We can only shake our heads in disbelief and wonder what mental aberration could bring a person to such a state—fabulously wealthy and yet starving in isolation. Unfortunately, some Christians are guilty of similar behavior. When God brings us into His family, we immediately become heir to a spiritual fortune. However, many ignore those resources, choosing instead to lead lives of frustration and defeat. A believer who fails to recognize those resources enjoys little more than spiritual bankruptcy.

In this first section of Ephesians, Paul provides an accounting of the spiritual blessings that we inherit due to our new position in Christ.

GOD HAS BLESSED US IN CHRIST
(Ephesians 1:1-3)

This book begins with an identification of the author (Paul the Apostle), the recipients (Ephesian believers), and an affirmation of the fact that salvation includes a wide range of spiritual blessings.

> **1. (1:1)** *The word* apostle *means "sent one." In the New Testament it is used of certain church leaders who had seen Christ personally. Who called Paul to become an apostle?*

> ❒ *"Saints" (literally "holy ones") refers to all who believe in Christ and have been born again through faith in Christ. How does Paul's use of the word saint differ from popular usage today?*

> ❒ *If we consciously think of ourselves as saints, how might it affect the way we live?*

2. (1:3) *What kinds of blessings has God given to you?*

GOD SAVED US (Ephesians 1:4-8)

S alvation and forgiveness of sin are only the beginning. Other riches include abundant spiritual wisdom and understanding.

1. (1:4) *When did God establish His plan for the salvation of humankind?*

❐ *Even though we do not always behave appropriately, what attributes does God see believers as possessing, based on Christ's righteousness?*

2. (1:5) *What does the concept of adoption communicate about our relationship with God through Jesus Christ?*

3. (1:6) *In what ways does our salvation bring praise to God?*

4. (1:7-8) List the blessings believers have received in Christ.

☐ On what basis have you received them?

☐ How does Paul describe God's attitude in giving spiritual blessings to us?

GOD GUIDES US (Ephesians 1:9-12)

*P*art of the understanding that believers receive is the revelation of God's will. Not only can we know God's purpose, we can also see how God accomplishes it through Jesus Christ.

1. (1:9-10) *In the New Testament, a "mystery" is something that we could not know unless God specifically revealed it to us. What is the <u>mystery</u> named in verse 10 that God has made known to us?*

mystery - Salvation of Jews + Gentiles. Romans 11:25 - Col 1:26.

How do we know God's will? ① Get in God's word Romans 12-15 / I Thess. 4-5 ② acceptance of it not guidance.

❏ When will all of the various elements in God's plan (including the church—Jew and Gentile becoming one) finally come to fruition and be understood?

2. (1:11) What was Paul's expectation about God's will being accomplished in the world?

3. (1:12) What "benefit" comes to God as a result of our response to Jesus Christ?

GOD SEALED US (Ephesians 1:13-14)

When we place our faith in Christ, we receive the Holy Spirit. Although the bulk of our inheritance is future, the Holy Spirit testifies to the fact that we will receive it.

1. (1:13) What must happen before a person can believe in Jesus Christ?

❏ What is the seal (security or proof of authenticity) that has been given to those who believe?

2. (1:14) *Earnest money is given when a person signs a contract. It is evidence that all of the terms of the contract will be met—that the individual will follow through on his promise. What is the "earnest" payment that we have received?*

❐ *What is the full inheritance of the believer?*

DIGGING DEEPER

1. *Since all believers are holy and blameless in our standing before God, how should this affect our actions and attitudes toward other Christians with whom we live and worship?*

❐ *In which of your relationships with other Christians should you realign some actions and attitudes?*

Relationships	**Changes I need to work on**
Church	
Home	

Relationships	**Changes I need to work on**
Extended Family	
Ministry	
Work	
Other _____	

2. Name some specific things that you can do to bring praise and glory to God this week.

Weekdays —

Saturday —

Sunday —

3. *How do believers' lives bring praise and glory to God in these situations:*

I Peter 3:14-17:

Philippians 4:18-20:

Titus 2:1-5:

Acts 16:14-15:

Romans 13:1-7:

4. *God offers us salvation through His Son Jesus Christ, but we must accept this gift. If you have accepted salvation, write a brief prayer of thanksgiving. If you have not yet accepted Jesus Christ, but would like to, write out a prayer thanking God for this gift. Tell Him that you believe Jesus Christ died for your sin, God raised Him from the dead, and that you accept salvation through Jesus.*

2

New Wisdom in Christ
EPHESIANS 1:15-23

When our family moved into our present house, every new day was an adventure. Each time we entered a room we discovered things that we had not realized before. Some parts of the house were just what we had expected; others were quite different.

Through the years we have become quite comfortable and accustomed to our unique house. We now take for granted the things that amazed and amused us initially. We don't even notice little things that a visitor might observe immediately.

In many ways the Christian life is similar. At first, everything is new and every discovery exciting. For new Christians, this section of Ephesians describes key features of life in Christ. But those of us who have been saved for some time may view this section differently. It reminds us of things we may be taking for granted. Whether we are new or seasoned Christians, the implications of our salvation are exciting. Ephesians 1:15-23 is the content of Paul's prayer for the Ephesians (and us), that we might understand all that God wants to give us.

FAITHFUL PRAYING FOR OTHER CHRISTIANS (Ephesians 1:15-16)

*P*aul participated in "long-distance" ministry to the Ephesian Christians. After hearing of their spiritual growth, Paul prayed regularly for them.

1. (1:15) *What two relationships in the Christian life was Paul concerned about?*

❑ *How is faith in Jesus Christ related to "love for all the saints"?*

THE IMPORTANCE OF WISDOM (Ephesians 1:17)

*O*ne specific request that Paul made for the Ephesians was that they would mature spiritually and come to know Christ better.

1. (1:17) *For a Christian, what should be the relationship between wisdom and God's revelation in Scripture?*

☐ *In what specific ways, thoughts, or actions might your life change if you always acted wisely, based on scriptural principles?*

THE IMPORTANCE OF SPIRITUAL UNDERSTANDING (Ephesians 1:18-21)

*P*aul prayed that the Ephesians would have spiritual insight to understand their hope, their wealth, and the power that God demonstrated through Christ.

1. (1:18-19) *What three things did Paul pray would result from having the eyes of their hearts enlightened?*

2. (1:19-20) *What example did Paul use to help explain the extent of God's great power?*

3. (1:20-21) *Describe how you feel about who Christ is, and the position He has, when you read these verses.*

THE EXTENT OF CHRIST'S AUTHORITY
(Ephesians 1:22-23)

God, through His power, has assigned to Christ a position of power and authority. Christ's authority is particularly important to the Church because He is our Head.

1. (1:22) *What are two ways in which God's power is seen in Jesus Christ?*

❐ *What do you think Paul means in this verse, that all things have been placed under the feet of Christ?*

2. (1:22-23) *Headship can imply two things—authority and giving direction. Both may be included here. What are some implications of the fact that Christ is Head of the church?*

3. (1:23) In what ways does Christ fill "all in all" (everything in every way)?

DIGGING DEEPER

1. Paul prayed regularly for the Ephesian believers (1:16). When do you pray regularly? For whom?

❐ What changes should you make in your prayer life?

2. Make a list of fellow believers and specific requests you would like to pray for this week. (Remember the types of requests Paul included in his prayer for the Ephesian believers.)

      Person   **_Request_**

1.

2.

3.

4.

3. *How did you feel about the truth of Christ's resurrection before you became a child of God through faith in Christ?*

❒ *What does it mean to you now?*

❒ *How does the fact of the future resurrection of all believers (I Corinthians 15:51-58) influence how you face the future?*

4. *Recall a time when you were aware of God's resurrection power (1:19) working in your life.*

❒ *In what areas of your life do you need to rely more on God's great power? It is available now for all who believe.*

❒ *What steps do you need to take to do this?*

❖

New Life in Christ
EPHESIANS 2:1-10

*I*t is easy to forget that two totally different systems are at work in the world. And these are in direct conflict with each other. We easily forget, even though we know, that God and Satan have nothing in common—that good and evil, light and dark, righteousness and unrighteousness are never in agreement. And because we forget, often we assume that there is a vast middle ground.

Scripture reveals that there is no neutral ground. One is either *for* God or opposed to Him. Paul describes these two systems in this first part of Ephesians 2. We all operated under Satan's system before we were saved—before we were made alive in Christ. But now that we have been born again, we should be operating on the basis of God's direction.

Of course, this means constant spiritual conflict because of Satan's influence in the world. We need only to listen to popular music or watch almost any TV program to become keenly aware of that conflict. Most of what is communicated through the secular media reflects distinctly anti-Christian values. And that means those presentations communicate principles that are appropriate to Satan's goals rather than God's.

But Paul's instruction in this section explains how we can live to glorify God through the power of His Holy Spirit. This is the power that "even when we were dead in sins, hath quickened us together with Christ" (2:5).

LIVING AS DEAD PEOPLE
(Ephesians 2:1-3)

*B*efore we became Christians, we were spiritually dead in sin. Our attitudes and actions were driven by earthly, physical desires which reflected Satan's purposes.

1. (2:1-2) *What are the characteristics of a person who is not alive spiritually?*

2. (2:2) *What is the relationship between Satan ("the prince of the power of the air") and "the course of this world"?*

3. (2:3) *What is the lifestyle of those who are dead (2:1) in their trespasses (literally, "false steps") and sins ("acts of missing the mark")?*

❒ *Name some specific ways the lifestyle of a Christian should be different.*

4. (2:3) *The phrase stating we were "by nature the children of wrath" (i.e. of God's wrath), is a Hebrew idiom asserting the essential depravity of human nature. This means that everyone, Jew and Gentile alike, stands guilty before God. What did we deserve for following Satan and for the way that we once lived?*

RECEIVING LIFE THROUGH CHRIST
(Ephesians 2:4-7)

As an expression of His love, God offers us life, saving us through His grace. And He also has given us countless other blessings along with salvation.

1. (2:4) *Why do you think God's love for us is so great?*

2. *"Grace" is God giving us something we don't deserve. "Mercy" is God* not *giving us what we* do *deserve. Contrast what God has given us (2:4-5) with what we deserve to be given (2:3).*

<u>**Ephesians 2:4-5**</u>　　　　　　<u>**Ephesians 2:3**</u>

23

❏ *In what ways has God been merciful to you?*

3. (2:5-6) What three things did God do for us as He demonstrated His great love in mercy?

4. (2:7) Why did God demonstrate His love for us so graciously?

LIVING TO GOD'S GLORY
(Ephesians 2:8-10)

Salvation is God's work, not our own, so we cannot brag about it. Now that we have been saved, it is our obligation to live in such a way that our works glorify God. This is what God planned for us long before we were saved.

1. (2:8) *What is the means of our salvation?*

2. (2:8-9) *What did we have to do in order to be saved?*

3. (2:8-10) *What is the proper relationship between faith and works in the Christian life?*

❐ *What "works" in your life bear testimony to the fact that you have been saved?*

4. (2:10) *What is meant by the phrase, "we are his [God's] workmanship"?*

❐ *When did God determine that we should do good works as an expression of our salvation?*

❐ *What are some of your good works that would show others what God has done in your life?*

DIGGING DEEPER

1. What can we do to resist unconsciously absorbing attitudes and copying the actions of those who follow "the prince of the power of the air"?

2. How should we respond to God in light of His great mercy expressed through His grace?

3. What are some reasons that a Christian might fail to live as God expects (doing good works)?

4. Paul wrote that God's resurrection power (Ephesians 1:19-20) is available to us. In Ephesians 2:6 he spoke of our having been spiritually resurrected with Christ. Look at Colossians 3:1-4 and Philippians 3:20. What additional instruction do you find for believers as "risen in Christ," and what do we have to look forward to?

New Relationships in Christ
EPHESIANS 2:11-22

*T*he daily newspaper can be very depressing reading. Terrorism, crime, and international conflict seem to dominate the news. Violence surrounds us, both in the form of aimless expressions of frustration or anger, and in coldly calculated attacks against specific persons or groups.

Much violence is motivated by religious fervor. Some of the most brutal wars in history were at least partially the result of religious disputes. Even today, religious issues are the source of much of the conflict that contributes to world tension.

Whether it be the continuing saga of conflict in the Middle East, ethnic cleansing in Europe, or bombings and shootings in Northern Ireland, the religious motivation is unmistakable. Yet, when a person becomes a member of God's family through faith in Jesus Christ, love rather than hatred should direct behavior. When love becomes the motivating factor, old conflicts and hostility are eliminated.

While "religion" alienates and divides people, biblical Christianity promotes peace and produces new unity. Instead of hating and fighting each other, those who have been in conflict are brought together into a single body, the body of Christ. This body grows and matures to the glory of God. And this new attitude of love should extend to those outside the body of Christ also.

HOPELESS SEPARATION
(Ephesians 2:11-12)

*B*efore placing their faith in Christ, Gentiles (the uncircumcised) were alienated from Israel (the circumcised) and from God. Their situation was hopeless, isolated from God and from His blessings.

1. (2:11) *The word* wherefore *refers back to the previous section. What Paul is about to say is built on the point he has just made. Reread 2:1-10 and summarize in a sentence or two the main idea of that section.*

2. (2:11-12) *What barriers separated Gentiles from Jews?*

Religious fervor - idea that they were unclean - uncircumsized. Not citizens.

❏ List the consequences of being a Gentile and not being part of the nation of Israel.

no citizenship
no hope / God in world

❏ How do you think the Gentile Christians felt when they heard verses 11 and 12 read aloud for the first time?

angry enough to fight
hopeless - tired of being left out.

JOYFUL RECONCILIATION — ABOLISH
(Ephesians 2:13) — CREATE - RECONCILE

*J*esus Christ, through His sacrificial death, enables those who were separated and alienated to come to God.

1. (2:13) To whom does Paul refer in the phrase, "Ye who sometimes were far off"? *Gentiles / Jews*

❏ How were they "made nigh" (reconciled) to God?

Jesus' shed blood.

2. In this passage, Paul describes reconciliation as being "made nigh" to God. Paul discussed this same concept in other New Testament letters. Read the Scripture passages listed and jot down the words or phrases that Paul uses to describe or define reconciliation.

Romans 5:6-11— died for sinners
justified.
reconciled by death of his son
rejoice in his love.

power
love

II Corinthians 5:14-21—
convinced 1 died for all
live not for self but for others
new creation. old gone, new has come
ministry of reconciliation. Ambassadors for Christ.

require moving from a worldly point of view

Colossians 1:21-23— in him
reconciled you through C death.
new hope - presented holy, free
from accusation - w/o blemish.

UNITY IN CHRIST (Ephesians 2:14-18)

*J*esus brought peace and reconciliation by destroying the wall between Jew and Gentile and establishing a new entity, the church. As a result, we all have equal access to God through faith in Jesus Christ. The metaphor describing the separation of Jews and Gentiles probably refers to the wall in the temple area which separated the Court of the Gentiles, the outermost court from the inner courts, open only to Jews.

ABOLISH

1. **(2:14)** What barrier was <u>removed</u> so that Jew and Gentile could become one?

The law + commandments that separating Jews + Gentiles.

2. **(2:15)** What is the "new man" to which Paul refers?

new church - Gentiles + Jews
"body" together

30

3. (2:15-16) *How and why was the barrier separating Jew and Gentile destroyed?* — To create 1 new body of believers — free of discord. *[Jesus' blood]* Reconciliation

❏ *Since Christ removed the barrier, why do you think there is still so much conflict between Jews and Gentiles?*
Pride — unable to see truth.

4. (2:17-18) *By what means do both Jew and Gentile have access to God the Father?* Through Jesus

POSITION IN GOD'S FAMILY (Ephesians 2:19-22)
Kingdom
Family
Temple

*N*ow all believers are part of the same group, the church. But what is the church? The church is built on the teachings of the apostles and prophets. Jesus Christ is the very Cornerstone of this teaching. The church is not a building made of wood, brick, or stone; it is all believers joined together in Him. Each believer is the very dwelling place of God's Holy Spirit, and together we grow in holiness.

1. (2:19) *List the words and/or phrases used to describe the Gentiles before and after they became Christians.*

foreigners   fellow citizens
aliens   God's people
              members of his
              household

2. (2:20) *A cornerstone is used to assure a level foundation. In ancient buildings, the entire structure was lined up with the chief cornerstone. Thus, its placement was crucial. How does this describe Christ, who is called the Chief Cornerstone?*

> Christ is Chief cornerstone + foundation is apostles + prophets. Christ is cornerstone holding Jews + Gentiles together.

3. (2:19-22) *Note the imagery Paul uses to describe the church. Using your imagination, explore more fully the metaphors Paul employs in these verses—citizens, family, temple. How closely does your local church resemble the picture Paul paints of the body of Christ?*

❏ *What changes would help it to become more like what Christ desires?*

> more trust
> more willingness to give whatever the cost, time, # talents to live God's chosen life for us.

4. (2:21-22) *How do you think additions are made to this holy temple so that it continues to grow and fit together?*

> growing together until as a body we raise up our "church" as a temple.

32

❏ *What do these verses suggest about relationships between Christians?* they should be nurturing, supportive + positive

DIGGING DEEPER

1. *Within modern culture, what are some of the identifiable groups that are hated by other groups? Why do they hate each other?* racial differences
- welfare community vs. working community
- liberal vs. conservative
- gay vs. traditional

❏ *How could a genuine relationship with Christ relieve this hostility?*

❏ *How should your relationship with Christ affect your life and relationships on a personal level?*

2. *What are some of the practical implications of the fact that all of us who are Christians have been "made nigh" (reconciled) to God?*

3. *In what situations have you personally experienced the peace that comes through Christ?*

☐ *How might you have responded to these situations if you were not a Christian?*

New Organism:
The Body of Christ
EPHESIANS 3:1-13

*T*he story is told about two small churches in a very small town. For years these churches had competed for the few townspeople who attended church regularly. Finally, someone suggested that rather than constantly struggling to outdo each other, they should merge into one congregation.

Most felt that this was an appropriate solution, so a committee was appointed to work out the details of the merger. The committee resolved many differences quite easily, and it appeared as though they would accomplish the transition with little trauma.

But a disagreement surfaced. Each congregation recited the Lord's Prayer in the morning worship service. Unfortunately, they recited different versions. One prayed "forgive us our debts as we forgive our debtors," while the other asked "forgive us our trespasses as we forgive those who trespass against us." While this seems to be a relatively minor variation, each congregation wanted to retain its version of the prayer. And the longer they worked to resolve the problem, the more each side became hardened and resistant to change. The disagreement became so intense that the appointed committee decided consolidation was impossible.

A brief notice in the local newspaper recounted the aborted attempt at consolidation. The newspaper's account explained the various issues surrounding the disagreement and the churches' inability to resolve it. The article concluded with this insightful remark: "After abandoning all hope of resolving the conflict, one church returned to its debts and the other to its trespasses."

How common such attitudes are among Christians! We forget all that we have in common and allow minor differences to paralyze us. But Paul clearly teaches in this section of Ephesians that we are "one body" in Jesus Christ. And this unity should enable us to represent Him effectively in the world.

REVELATION OF THE CHURCH
(Ephesians 3:1-6)

*I*n His grace, God revealed to Paul that during this age He was going to use a different means to express His eternal plan in the world. Through Christ, both Jew and Gentile have been brought together into one new entity, the church.

1. (3:1) *The phrase, "For this cause" directs our attention back to a previous point. Reread 2:11-22 and summarize the main point of that passage.*

2. (3:1-2) *To what group of people did Paul primarily direct his preaching?*

Gentiles

❏ *What do you think Paul meant when he described himself as a "prisoner of Jesus Christ" for the sake of the Gentiles?*

house arrest

3. (3:3-4) *Why was Paul given special insight?*

He was a Jew - who knew about the Gentiles - He could reach many

❏ *What are we to understand from his knowledge?*

God's hidden mystery will be made known to us.

4. (3:5) *A mystery, in the biblical sense, is something that could not be and had not been known before God specifically revealed it. Who, besides Paul, was able to understand this "mystery"?*

men in other generations apostles + prophets.

❏ *How was this mystery revealed?*

God's Holy Spirit.

5. (3:6) *The mystery revealed is that both Jew and Gentile become one in Christ. List the three major truths that are included in this mystery.*

1. *Gentiles are heirs w/ Israel*

2. *members of 1 body*

3. *Sharers of the promise of J.C.*

PAUL'S CONTRIBUTION TO BUILDING THE CHURCH (Ephesians 3:7-9)

*P*aul's ministry was to take the marvelous truth of the gospel to the Gentiles, though he felt unworthy of the honor. The inclusion of the Gentiles had always been a part of God's eternal plan, although not revealed previously. God commissioned Paul to communicate this truth clearly.

1. (3:7) *In this verse the word translated "minister" (servant) does not mean a slave but one who provides service, such as a waiter. What might it mean that Paul was made a minister/servant of this gospel?*

He was the mouthpiece to both.

❏ *What does verse 7 tell us about Paul's spirit and attitude?*

gift of grace

2. (3:8) *What are some of the reasons that Paul might have considered himself "less than the least of all saints"?*

He was a persecutor
speech problem

3. (3:8-9) *As a servant of the gospel, what two responsibilities were given to Paul?*

preach to Gentiles Christ's riches
reveal "mystery" to all

❏ *What information in verse 9 helps us to understand the "mystery" of the church?*

GOD'S PURPOSE FOR THE CHURCH
(Ephesians 3:10-13)

God intends for everyone to know what He is accomplishing. Through Christ, we can come to God freely and confidently.

1. (3:10) What is the purpose of the church according to this verse?

❏ Who needs to know about the "manifold (literally, multifaceted) wisdom of God"?

2. (3:11) Who is the focal point of God's eternal purpose?

3. (3:12) By what means may we approach God?

❏ For you, what does it mean to approach God with boldness and confidence?

4. (3:13) *Why do you think that Paul might have feared that the Ephesians were discouraged?*

❐ *Why were his tribulations their glory?*

DIGGING DEEPER

1. *If your church is functioning according to Ephesians 3:1-13, what qualities or traits should characterize it?*

2. *Why is unity among individuals so difficult to maintain?*

❐ *What forces hinder unity in your church?*

❏ What things could you (and others) do to promote unity in your church?

3. It's important to realize that we demonstrate Christ-honoring attitudes through our actions. What actions can you take this week to demonstrate an attitude of love and unity toward other Christians?

4. Since we can approach God freely and confidently, what traits should characterize our prayer lives?

❏ Our evangelistic efforts?

❖

6

New Power in Christ
EPHESIANS 3:14-21

❖

*T*he very mention of the word *housekeeping* strikes terror in the hearts of some people who are compulsive about cleanliness. A speck of dust, a cobweb, or a magazine out of place is, to them, a reflection of total depravity. While some maintain that cleanliness is next to godliness, these people put it ahead of godliness. They are the ones whose homes look like you could eat off the floor.

And then there are those whose living areas look as if someone *has been* eating off the floor! Somewhere between these two extremes is a balance. In our house, we are constantly working to achieve this balance of neat and clean (but not compulsively clean).

Elaine and some of her close friends often compare notes on the difficulty of maintaining balance in the mundane world of housekeeping. One year for Christmas one of these friends gave Elaine a framed motto which pictured a somewhat disheveled woman slumped in an easy chair. Below the picture was the phrase, "The secret of perfect housekeeping: very low standards." As you can imagine, this was a cherished gift from a dear friend.

Unfortunately, many apply a similar philosophy to living the Christian life. They set very low standards so that they have little to live up to. But God has already set the standards. His expectations for believers, as described in Ephesians 3:14-21, grow out of who He is and what Christ has done.

PRAY FOR SPIRITUAL STRENGTH
(Ephesians 3:14-17a)

*P*aul shares with the Ephesian believers his prayer for them, knowing that God's riches are available to His children. Paul specifically prayed that believers would experience the power that comes through giving Christ total possession of their lives.

1. (3:14) *While standing was the most common posture for prayer in the Old Testament, Paul suggests another position. What does the phrase, "I bow my knees unto the Father," indicate about Paul's attitude toward God?*

2. (3:15) *What is the relationship between God and the church (the body of Christ)?*

3. (3:16) *What resources does God use to provide us with strength for living?*

❏ *What do you think Paul meant when he expressed a desire for the Ephesians to be strengthened in their "inner man"?*

4. (3:17) *The word* dwell *is not used to emphasize physical location; rather, it connotes possession or control. What qualities would characterize someone who has Christ "dwelling in" (possessing) his or her heart?*

PRAY TO KNOW GOD'S LOVE FULLY
(Ephesians 3:17b-19)

*P*aul also prayed that believers, being grounded in the love of Christ, might grasp the scope of that love. We cannot understand this love except through God's revelation.

1. (3:17b) Note the verbs used here. What are the two ways in which Paul pictures believers? (Compare also I Corinthians 3:6 and Ephesians 2:20-22.)

2. (3:18) What are the four dimensions of the love of Christ that Paul describes?

❒ What do you think Paul intended to emphasize by using physical dimensions to describe an abstract concept such as love?

3. (3:19) What are some of the practical implications of having a fuller comprehension of Christ's love?

❑ *How can a believer show that he is filled with the love of God?*

DOXOLOGY OF PRAISE
(Ephesians 3:20-21)

Paul concludes his prayer with a glorious doxology to God. Paul praises God for what He does in our lives and for how His power works within us. And Paul prays that glory might come to God through Jesus Christ and through His body, the church, forever.

1. (3:20-21) Doxology *is a word built from two Greek words meaning "glory" and "words." In many churches, these verses are set to music and sung as a doxology. What do you see in them that makes them doxological?*

❑ *List some examples of how we as finite beings expect far less than the infinite God is able to accomplish.*

❏ How can we raise our expectation levels to agree more fully with God's power?

2. (3:20) While it is our responsibility to glorify God, we are not left to our own strength and wisdom in fulfilling this duty. According to this verse, what means does God use to accomplish His will in the world?

3. (3:21) How long will God continue to receive glory?

DIGGING DEEPER

1. In what areas do you think God's qualities or attributes need to be experienced more fully in your life?

❏ What specific steps can you take to gain a fuller understanding of Christ's love?

2. What impact do fighting and controversy among Christians have on the glory that God receives?

❏ In what ways do your interactions with other believers glorify God?

3. What do these Scriptures teach about giving glory to God?
John 15:8-10:

Isaiah 42:8:

I Corinthians 10:31:

Romans 15:5-7:

Romans 8:18:

Revelation 4:11:

4. Write out your personal paraphrase of Ephesians 3:20-21. Use these verses as your prayer to God.

"EVERYONE HAS A UNIQUE GIFT OF MINISTRY, AND MINE IS PARTICIPATING IN CHURCH FUND RAISERS."

Believers Ministering Faithfully
EPHESIANS 4:1-16

❖

*M*any years ago a well-known college football coach, returning to campus with his team, was asked a very unusual question by a reporter. "Tell me coach," the reporter asked, "what do you think football has done to improve the physical condition of America?"

"It has done absolutely nothing," the coach replied. "I define football as twenty-two men on the field desperately needing rest and twenty-two thousand in the stands desperately needing exercise."

This perceptive response certainly was unexpected, but its logic is inescapable. What most of us need is not another opportunity to watch superb athletes expend great physical energy. We need to burn some calories ourselves. And sitting on the sidelines, munching hot dogs and peanuts, is counterproductive.

The church faces a similar dilemma. We have a few players on the field desperately needing rest, with the vast majority sitting in the stands watching. Most pastors and other church leaders constantly face the problem of recruiting workers. Too few people are doing too many jobs. And too many people are watching them.

Christianity is not a spectator activity. It assumes involvement and participation by every member of Christ's body. Ephesians 4:1-16 is the classic passage describing the nature and strategy of the church. Though all Christians have much in common, we each make unique contributions. And only as everyone works can the body grow and thrive.

UNITY IN CHRIST'S BODY
(Ephesians 4:1-6)

As believers, we have an obligation to live out the doctrine that Paul communicated in the first three chapters of his letter to the Ephesians. We are to work at building and maintaining a strong, healthy church. This task is made easier because believers have seven significant elements in common.

> **1. (4:1)** *Since the word* therefore *refers back to chapters 1—3, it is important to understand these chapters. Briefly review them and write down several main ideas from Ephesians 1—3.*

2. (4:1) *Why do you think Paul described himself as "the prisoner of the Lord"?*

❏ *What is the main task on which Paul urged the Ephesians to focus their energy?*

3. (4:2) *What kinds of actions should result when a person is being humble and patient?*

4. (4:3) *What is the source of the unity that all believers possess?*

❏ *What will be the result when believers act in true unity?*

5. (4:4-6) *What seven things do all believers have in common as members of Christ, and what difference might these things make in our lives?*

| <u>Common Elements</u> | <u>Difference in Our Lives</u> |

DIVERSITY BASED ON CHRIST'S GIFTS (Ephesians 4:7-10)

While believers have much in common, each person is unique. Christ, who came to earth to die, rise again, and take His place as Head of the church, has given each of us special gifts of grace which enable us to serve Him.

1. (4:7) *"Grace" is sometimes translated "gifts of grace," referring to the special enabling for service given uniquely to every believer. What determines the allocation of grace that has been given to each believer?*

❑ *Who has received this special endowment for service?*

2. (4:8) *What two benefits come to believers, previously captives of sin and death, as a result of Christ's victorious resurrection from the dead?*

3. (4:9-10) *Ascending and descending probably mean burial in death (descending) and resurrection (ascending). How does Christ's willingness to come to earth and die set an example of humility and service for us (compare 4:2-3)?*

GROWTH OF THE BODY THROUGH MINISTRY (Ephesians 4:11-16)

Some have received key leadership gifts so that they can help others develop their gifts of service. It is important that each Christian serves to help build up the church, until everyone is mature, and that each Christian knows and practices biblical principles. This will promote growth and maturity in the body of Christ.

1. (4:11) *What are the four leadership gifts mentioned here?*

Foundational leadership gifts (see also 2:20):

1.

2.

Continuing leadership gifts:

3.

4.

2. (4:12) What is the task of those who have gifts of leadership?

☐ What happens to the body of Christ when God's people are prepared for and doing works of service?

3. (4:13) What two goals challenge believers to use their gifts of ministry?

☐ *Describe the result when Christians consistently use their ministry gifts.*

4. (4:14) *What is the main characteristic of an immature believer?*

5. (4:15) *What is the main characteristic of a mature believer?*

6. (4:16) *What happens to Christ's body when Christians minister regularly?*

DIGGING DEEPER

1. *What kinds of actions contribute to maintaining the unity that we have as believers?*

2. Notice that all three members of the Godhead are mentioned in verses 3-6. How does the unity of the Trinity provide an example for believers' unity?

3. What would happen in our churches if every believer recognized that he or she has been given a special enabling for service?

❐ What part can you play in promoting the recognition and implementation of this truth?

4. In your church, who has been given leadership gifts and how are they being exercised?

5. The body only achieves maximum potential when every individual part of that body functions effectively. What is your role in building up the body of Christ? (See also I Corinthians 12:4-11 and Romans 12:3-8.)

❖

"Then one day he stopped lying and cheating, and everyone could see that his life had been changed. Can they have a book like this in a public library?"

Believers Living Holy Lives
EPHESIANS 4:17-32

❖

*O*ne characteristic of our society is the incredible bombardment of carefully conceived media advertising. Every day we are subjected to thousands of brief, penetrating messages designed to captivate and motivate us. Advertisers want to stake a claim in the corners of our minds so that we will feel a need for, and look favorably on, their products when it comes time to make a purchase.

We often find the strategies and techniques that ad agencies employ both fascinating and instructive. TV commercials, for example, often exhibit more originality and creativity than the shows which they interrupt. Certainly more money is spent per minute in producing the commercials than on most entertainment shows.

One of the advertising techniques that seems to have fallen into disfavor in recent years is the "before and after" testimonial. Perhaps this is due to the potential abuse of such a technique. Recently, we observed a before/after advertisement for a diet program. The "before" photo was poorly lit, out of focus, the person looked sad and was dressed in sloppy clothing. In the "after" photo the lighting and focus were excellent, the person was well-groomed, smiling, and dressed fashionably. The difference was more in the photo than in the person!

One area where the before/after technique should be totally valid is our Christian experience. The quality of life after conversion should show a radical departure from our old lives. Paul paints a graphic word picture of the Christian's "before and after" experience in the second half of chapter four.

CHARACTERISTICS OF OUR OLD LIFE
(Ephesians 4:17-19)

*C*hristians should not live as they did when they were unsaved. Their mental focus was self-centered, their hearts hardened to God, and they were driven to participate in evil behavior.

1. (4:17) *What does the phrase about living "not as other Gentiles" suggest about the Ephesians' lifestyle prior to their conversion?*

2. (4:17-18) *Throughout this section of the letter, Paul uses the word* Gentile *to describe the Ephesians before salvation. However,* Gentile *can be understood also, in a more general* *reference, to anyone who lives in rebellion against God. What traits are characteristic of what Paul calls "Gentile thinking"?*

3. (4:18) *Describe the relationship between a "blindness [hardening] of heart," "ignorance," and "darkened understanding."*

4. (4:19) *What is the result of a hardened heart?*

❑ *In this verse Paul summarizes a pagan lifestyle. List the three words that characterize this lifestyle.*

5. *In what ways does Gentile society, as described in verses 17-19, appear similar to modern society?*

CONTRAST WITH NEW LIFE
(Ephesians 4:20-24)

*B*elievers came to know Christ through understanding and accepting the truth. And this truth includes instruction on how we ought to live. This means turning our backs on our old style of life and being made new creatures, modeled after God in righteousness and holiness.

1. (4:20) *What does the phrase "so learned" mean?*

2. (4:21) *What was the way in which the Ephesians came to know Christ?*

3. (4:22) *What are the characteristics (motivations, drives, and attitudes) of the "old man"?*

4. (4:23-24) *How should a person act when God has given him or her a new mind?*

CULTIVATING GODLY ACTIONS AND ATTITUDES (Ephesians 4:25-32)

As believers, our lives should be characterized by godly behavior in five different areas. These include telling the truth, controlling anger, not stealing, talking in a wholesome manner, and avoiding improper attitudes and speech. We should be kind, compassionate, and forgiving.

1. (4:25) *The word* wherefore *points back to the verses immediately preceding it. Summarize the main points of the previous passage (4:20-24).*

2. (4:25) *What should a Christian stop doing and start doing?*

❏ *What is the reason for this command?*

3. (4:26) *What are the proper and improper ways of handling anger?*

4. (4:27) *What is the reason for this approach to anger?*

5. (4:28) *How should Christians act and not act regarding material possessions?*

❐ *What is the reason for this attitude toward material possessions?*

6. (4:29) *What should and should not characterize a Christian's talk?*

❐ *What will be the result of godly communication?*

7. (4:29-32) *The final exhortation seems especially relevant for today's churches. What results (verse 30) from relationships characterized by bitterness (animosity, jealousy), wrath (outbursts of temper), anger, clamor (brawling, shouting, arguing), evil speaking (slander, injuring reputation, gossip), and malice (ill will, hoping for another's hurt)?*

8. (4:32) What positive actions should characterize our relationships?

DIGGING DEEPER

1. What specific things can you do to keep from hardening your heart, becoming calloused, and losing sensitivity?

❐ *What role should the Word of God play in helping to maintain your sensitivity and avoiding a hardened heart?*

2. When someone becomes a Christian, that person's whole life (world-view, thought processes, actions, attitudes, etc.) is changed. Why do you think that many who claim to be Christians seem to think and act more like "Gentiles" than new creations in Christ?

3. Reread the six exhortations in 4:25-32. Which ones are most needed in our churches? Why? (Notice, in all of these exhortations, Paul stresses that what we do affects others.)

4. Chapter 4 ends with an emphasis on relating to others as God related to us. Are there people who have offended you? How? Who are they?

❑ What should you do about these offenses?

❑ How can you demonstrate a Christ-like attitude toward these people?

5. Take a few minutes to pray and ask God to help you understand which of these exhortations apply most directly to you. Write down how you want God to help you deal with these problems.

❖

9

"BECAUSE YOU'RE SUPPOSED TO BE A <u>VISIBLE</u> REPRESENTATION OF CHRIST IN THE WORLD. THAT'S WHY YOU HAVE TO TAKE A BATH."

Believers Living Morally Pure Lives
EPHESIANS 5:1-14

❖

A Christian friend of ours wanted to share what Jesus Christ meant to her with her friends and co-workers. Unfortunately, she worked for a company that did not look kindly on religious conversations at work.

Our friend, who lived far from her place of work, had no outside contact with her work associates. So she prayed that somehow God would give her an opportunity to talk to them about Jesus Christ.

One day as she was leaving work, another employee approached her, asking if they could talk. This person was facing major problems in her life and felt as though she couldn't cope. She said that she could tell our friend was different from the others who worked there. She didn't know what made our friend different, but she knew she wanted what our friend had.

They stopped for a cup of coffee in a nearby restaurant where our friend was able to lead her co-worker to Christ. That night, the long ride home seemed shorter as she rejoiced in God's answer to her prayer.

In Ephesians 5, Paul reminds us that we who have accepted Christ are the visible representations of Christ in this world. We are to shine as lights illuminating a dark world. And as we shine as lights, we will see results in our lives and the lives of others.

WALK IN LOVE (Ephesians 5:1-2)

*B*elievers are admonished to model their lives after God and to practice love, just as Jesus Christ, who willingly gave Himself for us.

1. (5:1) *Who should believers follow (literally, "imitate")?*

❒ *What relationship with God do we have that enables us to imitate Him?*

2. (5:2) *Is the example of Jesus Christ more tangible and understandable than the example of God the Father? How?*

❒ *A "sweetsmelling savour" offering refers to the Old Testament where a sacrifice was a pleasant aroma to God* because it indicated the offerer's faith. What did it mean for Jesus Christ to express His love for us?

WALK IN MORAL PURITY (Ephesians 5:3-6)

God's children should avoid all sexual impurity (and other vices) and be characterized by thanksgiving. Only those who have been cleansed by God can be part of God's kingdom; all others are doomed to wrath.

1. (5:3-6) *Our language reflects our culture's social values. Today, many equate love with sex. But "love" (5:2) is sacrificing for another's benefit, and Paul clearly taught that sexual immorality is the opposite of love. List the kinds of behavior that are inappropriate for believers.*

2. (5:3-4) *How does giving thanks (expressing appreciation) contrast with the sins listed?*

3. (5:5) *This verse does not refer to a person who periodically sins, but one who is driven by ungodly desires. Such a person has not accepted Christ's sacrifice (5:2).*

According to verse 5, what behaviors characterize the ungodly person whom Paul describes here?

4. (5:6) *Apparently, there were some who falsely taught that you could say you followed Christ but do anything you wanted. Rather than inheriting eternal life, what will be the end reward of those who follow such false teaching?*

WALK IN THE LIGHT (Ephesians 5:7-14)

Christians should never join with others in sin as they might have in the past. Our light can only shine as we demonstrate God-honoring behavior. Rather than participating in sin, we should expose it in the light of God's holiness shining out through us.

1. (5:7) *What should a Christian's attitude be toward false teachers and those who rationalize sin?*

2. (5:8) *What do you think it means when Paul says that once believers were darkness but now they are light?*

3. (5:9) *Paul uses the analogy of light enabling a plant to bear good fruit. By contrast, darkness (5:11) bears no fruit. What fruit should be the outcome of living as children of light?*

❐ *Give specific examples of how you can walk as a child of light.*

4. (5:10) *How can we find out what is acceptable to the Lord?*

5. (5:11-12) *What should a believer's attitude be toward the fruitless deeds of darkness?*

6. (5:13-14) *What exposes the deeds of those who are ungodly, living disobedient lives?*

7. (5:14) *In what way has light (truth) awakened, or made alive, a believer in Christ?*

DIGGING DEEPER

1. *Recall some times when you have seen young children imitating their parents. Then, list some specific ways that we, as God's children, can imitate Christ.*

2. *Compare this Ephesians passage with I John 3:14-18. If Christ's love extended even to giving His life for us, what should loving each other mean to us?*

3. *How can believers shine as light in the world and yet not drive away those who live in darkness?*

4. Consider the nine-fold fruit of the Spirit (Galatians 5:22-23). What are ways that each of these qualities can be seen in your life?

Love—

Joy—

Peace—

Longsuffering (Patience)—

Gentleness (Kindness)—

Goodness—

Faith (Faithfulness)—

Meekness (Power under control)—

Temperance (Self-Discipline)—

❖

"MY PARENTS SHARE THE FAMILY ECONOMIC BURDEN EQUALLY. DAD SCRIMPS AND MOM SAVES."

Believers Reflecting Spirit-Filled Lives
EPHESIANS 5:15-33

❖

*I*nstead of leading truly balanced lives, many people swing from one extreme to another, just like a pendulum.

We have a friend who had been a pretty good athlete when he was younger. But the responsibilities of family and vocation, combined with too much food and too little exercise, had taken their toll.

One summer day we saw him laboring down the street, puffing like an asthmatic water buffalo. He was soaked with perspiration and glowed a brilliant shade of red. Between gasps he explained that he had decided to get back into shape and had just run five miles. From the extreme of a sedentary life he had swung, like a pendulum, to the other extreme—fitness fanatic.

People frequently go to extremes when discussing Paul's instructions to families. Some distort Paul's teaching to promote suppression of women or other groups. Others argue just as vehemently to try to explain away Paul's teachings. What we need is balance.

Every one of us functions in a variety of relationships. In order to experience God's blessing, we must look for ways to promote others, rather than ourselves. Fighting for our rights is carnality. Relinquishing them (submitting) for the good of others is spirituality.

LIVING IN SPIRIT-FILLED SUBMISSION (Ephesians 5:15-21)

*E*ach Christian should live carefully and wisely before God. We should allow the Holy Spirit to control our lives. We demonstrate this control by the way we speak to each other, the way we speak to God, an attitude of thanksgiving, and submitting to others.

1. (5:15) *Based on this verse, how should believers live (act)?*

❑ *What do you think it means to live as a wise person rather than a foolish person?*

2. (5:16) *How does this exhortation to make the most of every opportunity "because the days are evil" relate to verses 11-14?*

❒ *Name one way you can apply this exhortation in your life.*

3. (5:18) *What should and should not control our lives?*

4. (5:19) *For believers, personally indwelt by the Holy Spirit, what should characterize our conversation with each other?*

5. (5:19) *Notice that singing is a heart response. Even those who think they can't sing aloud can sing in their hearts. To whom should spiritual music be directed?*

6. (5:20) *What should be our attitude toward all circumstances that we encounter?*

7. (5:21) *What attitude should we demonstrate toward others if the Holy Spirit controls us?*

BEHAVIOR OF SPIRIT-FILLED WIVES (Ephesians 5:22-24)

A wife should submit to her husband as evidence of her heart-service to God because the husband is head of his wife as Christ is Head of the church. As the church submits to Christ, so should a Christian wife submit to her own husband.

1. (5:22) *A wife demonstrates spiritual maturity by placing her husband's welfare ahead of her own. This is a decision she makes, not something her husband forces her to do. When a wife does this, to whom is she really submitting?*

2. (5:23) *Why should a wife submit to her own husband?*

❐ Headship and submission do not imply superiority and inferiority. They explain functional relationships as a student submits to a teacher. This passage does not imply that all women should submit to all men, but describes relationships in a marriage. What is the parallel between a husband and Christ?

❐ As the Head of the church, what did Christ do for the church, His body?

3. (5:24) What is the parallel between a wife and the church?

BEHAVIOR OF SPIRIT-FILLED HUSBANDS (Ephesians 5:25-33)

A Christian husband will love his wife as Christ loved the church, giving himself totally for her. Also, a husband should love his wife as he loves his own body and cares for it because she is part of his body. Just as there is a profound relationship between Christ and the church, so also must a husband and wife relate.

1. (5:25, compare 5:21) How does a husband (out of reverence for God) "submit" himself to his wife?

2. (5:25) *How did Christ show His love for the church?*

3. (5:26-27) *What are some of the things that Christ has done for the church?*

4. (5:28-30) *It is normal and natural for a man to care for, nurture, and protect his own body. Why should a husband treat his wife as he treats his own body?*

5. (5:31) *This verse probably refers to Genesis 2:18-25. What are some of the implications of a husband and wife being one flesh, especially regarding the quality and duration of the marriage relationship?*

6. (5:32-33) How does Paul summarize his advice to husbands and wives?

DIGGING DEEPER

1. How can you specifically practice these four qualities of the Christian life (5:19-21)?

Speaking to one another spiritually:

Making music to God:

Thanking God for all things:

Submitting to each other:

2. What are some practical ways in which a wife can relate to her husband as the church relates to Christ?

3. What are some practical ways in which a husband can love his wife as Christ loved the church, and as he loves his own body?

4. As an expression of spiritual maturity, every believer is to submit in certain relationships (5:21). Submitting means to place another's welfare or preferences ahead of our own. The first New Testament occurrence of the word submit is Luke 2:51, when Jesus subordinated His personal preference to His parents'. Compare also I Corinthians 11:3, and summarize what we learn about submission from these passages.

5. Reread Ephesians 5:15-33. Write several sentences explaining what you think these verses teach us about living the Christian life as a personal dwelling place of God's Holy Spirit.

"NO, DEAR. WE WOULDN'T WANT TO ASK GOD'S BLESSING ON THE WORK OF THE DEVIL, BUT BRUSSELS SPROUTS AREN'T THE WORK OF THE DEVIL."

Believers Obeying the Spirit
EPHESIANS 6:1-9

❖

*O*ne of the most important concerns for parents in any society is guiding children into mature, productive adulthood. This means helping them to develop appropriate values that will guide them in making good judgments and decisions.

Some years ago, researchers at a major university did a longitudinal study of delinquent behavior. They observed children as they progressed from infancy to adulthood. As a result of years of study, they were able to isolate some factors contributing to delinquent behavior. By observing a preschool child in his environment, they could predict teen delinquent behavior with almost 95 percent accuracy.

The researchers found that consistent discipline, particularly from the father, was the key factor in avoiding delinquent behavior. Of the three styles they identified—strict, moderate, and lax—they found that moderate (consistent) discipline was best. Surprisingly, they found that strict discipline was worst. Because strict discipline often is harsh, and because consistency is so difficult with strict discipline, it usually proves counterproductive. The children become discouraged and give up.

In this passage, Paul has much to say to parents about how they relate to children. And he also speaks to us about other relationships.

BEHAVIOR OF SPIRIT-CONTROLLED CHILDREN (Ephesians 6:1-3)

Children must obey their parents. This command in the New Testament carries the same promise as given in the Old Testament: a long life to those who obey.

1. (6:1) *Why is it right for children to obey their parents?*

2. (6:1-2) *How do obedience and honoring father and mother fit together with a child's obligation to God?*

3. *While the second commandment (Exodus 20:5-6) includes a general consequence, this is the first commandment with a* *specific promise. What outcomes would you expect from obeying the command in 6:2?*

4. (6:3) *What are the implied consequences of a disobedient, undisciplined life?*

BEHAVIOR OF SPIRIT-CONTROLLED PARENTS (Ephesians 6:4)

*P*arents have obligations, too. Parents should rear their children with God's training and instruction and not exasperate them.

1. (6:4) *"Fathers" are addressed here not because they alone are responsible, but rather because of their leadership responsibility (5:23-24). What should fathers do to ensure that their children are brought up in the training and instruction of the Lord?*

❏ *What kinds of parental attitudes and actions would tend to exasperate (provoke to wrath) children?*

❏ *"Training" (nurture) includes guidance, direction, and encouragement. "Instruction" (admonition) emphasizes correction. How do guiding and correcting both play a part in child-rearing?*

❏ *In what sense does the way we rear our children come from God?*

BEHAVIOR OF SPIRIT-CONTROLLED WORKERS (Ephesians 6:5-8)

Christian slaves were to respond to their masters as they would to Christ, not just to please them but to honor God. They—and we—should work knowing that God is in control and ultimately will reward. Principles that applied to first-century servants relate to employees today.

1. (6:5) *What attitude should workers today have as they serve their employers?*

2. (6:6) *Who watches over those working for masters?*

3. (6:6-7) *Obviously a slave would want his master to think well of him, but Paul goes beyond this in suggesting higher motivation. What explanation does Paul give for his exhortation to serve appropriately?*

4. (6:8) *What is the end result or outcome of faithful service?*

5. *Based on verses 5-8, what appropriate guidelines could you suggest for workers today?*

❒ *What areas or attitudes do you need to change?*

❒ *How do you honor Christ at work?*

BEHAVIOR OF SPIRIT-CONTROLLED MASTERS (Ephesians 6:9)

*P*aul ends this section on "submitting one to another" (5:21) with an exhortation to masters. A Christian master (boss) must treat his slaves sensitively, knowing that God is his Master and He does not play favorites.

1. (6:9) *What is referred to by the phrase, "the same things"?*

2. (6:9) *What reasons does Paul give for not threatening slaves (employees)?*

❏ *What do you think Paul would say about the use of intimidation or coercion in motivating workers?*

❏ *Notice that Paul never implies that Christ removes differences in position or function. He does state that all should be valued equally as persons. How does the last phrase in verse 9 fit together with verse 8?*

DIGGING DEEPER

1. *What can parents do to help their children follow God's instructions to them in this passage?*

❐ *How could the example of Jesus' earthly life (compare Luke 2:52 and Hebrews 5:8) help parents DO THIS?*

2. *What were some of your parents' attitudes/actions that "exasperated" you as a child?*

❐ *What suggestions would you offer to help parents avoid exasperating their children?*

3. *In what ways are today's employees both similar to, and different from, slaves?*

❏ What expectations does Christ have of you as an employee?

4. What suggestions would you give to employers (supervisors) to help them effectively lead those who report to them?

5. Reread Ephesians 6:1-9. Then write down all the general guidelines for relationships that you can find in these verses.

> "I HAVE THE POWER TO OVERCOME SATAN IN ANY FORM HE TAKES, EVEN LONG DIVISION.
> "I HAVE THE POWER TO OVERCOME SATAN IN ANY FORM HE TAKES, EVEN LONG DIVISION.
> I HAVE...."

Believers Living With Spiritual Power
EPHESIANS 6:10-24

❖

When our first son was very young, we discussed the traits that we wanted to cultivate in our children (and in ourselves, too). At the top of our list was honesty. If our sons could learn to be honest with God, with us, and others, then they could be honest with themselves. And so we worked at encouraging this and other character traits.

Interestingly, we soon discovered that certain values we were trying to teach seemed contradictory. We wanted them to be honest always, but we were horrified when one of our young sons made a very unkind, but true, comment to a hostess in a home where we were visiting. And so we had to teach discretion. It is wrong to lie, but being truthful doesn't mean you have to say everything you think.

We also wanted our sons to be creative and imaginative when approaching tasks and opportunities. But sometimes school teachers and others in positions of responsibility placed a higher value on conformity and compliance than on creativity and innovation. So we tried to stimulate our sons to view life with freshness, but also to avoid "rocking the boat" needlessly.

Nowhere does the tension become more obvious than when teaching both independence and cooperation. We all need to work and function as strong, self-sufficient individuals. God has given us many resources to use for His glory.

But we are also members of the body of Christ—accountable to, and responsible for, each other.

In this final section of Ephesians, Paul stresses both aspects of the Christian life. And the tension between independence and cooperation also produce tension here. But we do not have to stand alone. The rest of the body of Christ is there to assist us as we strive to live victoriously. God provides us with the resources to conquer Satan in his attacks.

EQUIPPED FOR SPIRITUAL CONFLICT (Ephesians 6:10-17)

*I*n order to be strong, we need to arm ourselves against Satan. Since we are engaged in spiritual battle, we need to be protected with spiritual armor: truth, righteousness, a foundation for our feet, a shield, a helmet, and a sword.

1. (6:10)   *What is the source of a believer's strength?*

2. (6:11-12) *The pieces of armor to which Paul refers as he describes spiritual preparation were worn by Roman soldiers. Why is it important for Christians to be spiritually prepared?*

3. (6:13) *What is the result of being clothed in spiritual armor?*

4. (6:14) *Truth here refers to telling the truth. Why is personal honesty important in standing against Satan?*

❒ *Righteousness is the quality of righteous or holy living. What does righteous living mean to a believer?*

5. (6:15) *Having feet shod is for the purpose of standing firm with stability, not for moving forward. Why is standing firm on the gospel of peace important to a believer engaged in spiritual battle?*

❒ *How can a Christian have peace in the midst of conflict?*

6. (6:16) What part does our faith (which is the actual shield) play in our defense against Satan and his attacks?

7. (6:17) How does salvation protect or influence our minds?

☐ The sword is the only offensive element in this list of the Christian's armor. Why is practical knowledge of the Word of God important to every believer?

SUPPORTING OTHERS IN SPIRITUAL CONFLICT (Ephesians 6:18-20)

We are responsible to pray for others so that they also can live effectively. Paul knew how crucial this intercession was in his life.

1. (6:18) What part does prayer play in successfully withstanding Satan's attacks?

❏ *What do you think Paul meant when he admonished the believers to be alert ("watching")?*

2. (6:19-20) *What did Paul want his fellow believers to pray about for him?*

❏ *What is the importance of praying these same requests for other Christians today?*

CONCLUSION AND BLESSING (Ephesians 6:21-24)

*T*ychicus was to tell the Ephesians what had happened to Paul (probably while delivering the letter) and to encourage them with a personal word. Paul's final encouragement included a prayer for them to experience the peace, grace, and love of God.

1. (6:21) *Tychicus often worked with Paul, frequently as a messenger. What were some personal qualities of Tychicus?*

2. (6:21-22) What did Paul want Tychicus to do for him?

❒ How would knowing Paul's condition encourage the believers?

DIGGING DEEPER

1. How should we prepare ourselves daily if we recognize that we are engaged in spiritual battle, not simply a physical one?

2. What do you need to do in order to use the sword of the Spirit effectively in life's battles?

3. What are some ways that Christians help and encourage each other to stand strong in spiritual battle?

4. *List some fellow Christians—both near and far away—for whom you need to be more faithful and effective in prayer:*

☐ *How can you be more consistent in interceding for them in their spiritual battles?*

5. *As you think about the spiritual armor God has given you, what specific attacks of Satan does each repel in your life?*
girdle of truth —

breastplate of righteousness —

feet shod with gospel of peace —

shield of faith —

helmet of salvation —

sword of Spirit —

6. *Based on what you have learned from Ephesians, what specific areas would you ask God to strengthen in your life?*